—— Words of ——
FAITH

Original edition published in English under the title
Words of Faith by Lion Publishing, Tring, England,
copyright © 1974 Lion Publishing.

First published in the United States and Canada in
1983 by Thomas Nelson Publishers.

Published in Nashville, Tennessee, by Thomas Nelson,
Inc. and distributed in Canada by Lawson Falle, Ltd.,
Cambridge, Ontario.

Photographs by Lion Publishing/David Alexander.

Scripture quotations are from the *Good News Bible*—Old
Testament: Copyright © American Bible Society 1976;
New Testament: Copyright © American Bible Society
1966, 1971, 1976.

ISBN 0-8407-5333-0

Words of
FAITH

Thomas Nelson Publishers
Nashville • Camden • New York

THE LORD MY SHEPHERD

The Lord is my shepherd;
I have everything I need.
He lets me rest in fields of green grass
and leads me to quiet pools of fresh water.
He gives me new strength.
He guides me in the right paths,
as he has promised.
Even if I go through the deepest darkness,
I will not be afraid, Lord,
for you are with me.
Your shepherd's rod and staff protect me.

You prepare a banquet for me,
where all my enemies can see me;
you welcome me as an honored guest
and fill my cup to the brim.
I know that your goodness and love will be
with me all my life;
and your house will be my home as long
as I live.

PSALM 23

An Eastern shepherd leads his sheep in the hills of Judea.

ALL DAY LONG I TRUST IN YOU

To you, O Lord, I offer my prayer;
in you, my God, I trust.
Save me from the shame of defeat;
don't let my enemies gloat over me!
Defeat does not come to those who trust in you,
but to those who are quick to rebel against you.

Teach me your ways, O Lord;
make them known to me.
Teach me to live according to your truth,
for you are my God, who saves me.
I always trust in you.

PSALM 25:1–5

Two donkey-riders on a track through the stony landscape of southern Israel.

8

AT NIGHT, A QUIET MIND

There are many who pray:
"Give us more blessings, O Lord.
Look on us with kindness!"
But the joy that you have given me is more than
they will ever have with all their grain and wine.
When I lie down, I go to sleep in peace;
you alone, O Lord, keep me perfectly safe.

PSALM 4:6–8

Mediterranean breakers reflect the setting sun.

I WAKE UP SAFE

You, O Lord, are always my shield from
danger;
you give me victory
and restore my courage.
I call to the Lord for help,
and from his sacred hill he answers me.

I lie down and sleep,
and all night long the Lord protects me.
I am not afraid of the thousands of enemies who
surround me on every side.

PSALM 3:3–6

A gazelle at Ein Gedi, where David hid from his enemies.

GOD'S PROMISES

"But now I will come," says the Lord,
"because the needy are oppressed
and the persecuted groan in pain.
I will give them the security they long for."
The promises of the Lord can be trusted;
they are as genuine as silver
refined seven times in the furnace.

PSALM 12:5–6

Light at the end of a dark tunnel in the ruins of the Roman
theatre at Miletus.

NEW CONFIDENCE

I love the Lord, because he hears me;
he listens to my prayers.
He listens to me
every time I call to him.
The danger of death was all around me;
the horrors of the grave closed in on me;
I was filled with fear and anxiety.
Then I called to the Lord,
"I beg you, Lord, save me!"

The Lord is merciful and good;
our God is compassionate.
The Lord protects the helpless;
when I was in danger, he saved me.
Be confident, my heart,
because the Lord has been good to me.

PSALM 116:1–7

Guy-ropes on a bedouin tent in the desert.

I WILL NOT BE AFRAID

The Lord is my light and my salvation;
I will fear no one.
The Lord protects me from all danger;
I will not be afraid.

When evil men attack me and try to kill me,
they stumble and fall.
Even if a whole army surrounds me,
I will not be afraid;
even if enemies attack me,
I will still trust God. . .

In times of trouble he will shelter me;
he will keep me safe in his Temple
and make me secure on a high rock.
So I will triumph over my enemies around me.
With shouts of joy I will offer sacrifices in
his Temple;
I will sing, I will praise the Lord.

PSALM 27:1–3, 5–6

A lighthouse at the port of Jaffa, ancient Joppa, seen above
the houses and alleys of the old town.

MY SHELTER

You are my refuge and defense;
guide me and lead me as you have promised.
Keep me safe from the trap that has been
set for me;
shelter me from danger.
I place myself in your care.
You will save me, Lord;
you are a faithful God.

You hate those who worship false gods;
but I trust in you.
I will be glad and rejoice
because of your constant love.
You see my suffering;
you know my trouble.
You have not let my enemies capture me;
you have given me freedom to go where I wish . . .

How wonderful are the good things
you keep for those who honor you!
Everyone knows how good you are, how
securely you protect those who trust you.

PSALM 31:3–8, 19

A farm and fields in the Syrian desert near Aleppo.

IN GOD'S SAFE-KEEPING

Whoever goes to the Lord for safety,
whoever remains under the protection of the
Almighty,
can say to him,
"You are my defender and protector.
You are my God; in you I trust."

He will keep you safe from all hidden dangers
and from all deadly diseases.
He will cover you with his wings;
you will be safe in his care;
his faithfulness will protect and defend you.
You need not fear any dangers at night
or sudden attacks during the day
or the plagues that strike in the dark
or the evils that kill in daylight.

PSALM 91:1–6

On the road from Jerusalem to Jericho, formerly notorious for
bandits, and scene of Jesus' story of the Good Samaritan.

WHEN I AM AFRAID

When I am afraid, O Lord Almighty,
I put my trust in you.
I trust in God and am not afraid; I praise him for
what he has promised.
What can a mere human being do to me? . . .

You know how troubled I am;
you have kept a record of my tears.
Aren't they listed in your book?
The day I call to you,
my enemies will be turned back.
I know this: God is on my side—the Lord,
whose promises I praise.
In him I trust, and I will not be afraid.
What can a mere human being do to me?
O God, I will offer you what I have promised;
I will give you my offering of thanksgiving,
because you have rescued me from death
and kept me from defeat.
And so I walk in the presence of God,
in the light that shines on the living.

PSALM 56:3–4, 8–13

The sun seen through the branches of an acacia, one of the
few trees to grow in the desert.

24

WHEN I AM ANXIOUS

Lord, how happy is the person you instruct,
the one to whom you teach your law!
You give him rest from days of trouble until a pit
is dug to trap the wicked . . .

Who stood up for me against the wicked?
Who took my side against the evildoers?
If the Lord had not helped me,
I would have gone quickly to the land of silence.
I said, "I am falling";
but your constant love, O Lord, held me up.
Whenever I am anxious and worried,
you comfort me and make me glad.

PSALM 94:12–13, 16–19

A track through deep shadow in the mountains of Samaria.

MY HELP COMES FROM THE LORD

I look to the mountains;
where will my help come from?
My help will come from the Lord,
who made heaven and earth.

He will not let you fall;
your protector is always awake.
The protector of Israel
never dozes or sleeps.
The Lord will guard you;
he is by your side to protect you.
The sun will not hurt you during the day,
nor the moon during the night.

The Lord will protect you from all danger;
he will keep you safe.
He will protect you as you come and go
now and forever.

PSALM 121

The moon over the mountains of Lebanon, still streaked with
snow in the late spring.

NEVER SHAKEN

Those who trust in the Lord are like Mount
Zion,
which can never be shaken, never be moved.
As the mountains surround Jerusalem,
so the Lord surrounds his people,
now and forever.

PSALM 125:1–2

On "Mount Zion", the hill on which Jerusalem was built, the
walls of the ancient Temple area still stand today.

GOD IS WITH US

God is our shelter and strength,
always ready to help in times of trouble.
So we will not be afraid, even if the earth is
shaken
and mountains fall into the ocean depths;
even if the seas roar and rage,
and the hills are shaken by the violence.

There is a river that brings joy to the city of God,
to the sacred house of the Most High.
God is in that city, and it will never be
destroyed;
at early dawn he will come to its aid.
Nations are terrified, kingdoms are shaken;
God thunders, and the earth dissolves.

The Lord Almighty is with us;
the God of Jacob is our refuge.

PSALM 46:1–7

Soon after its source, the River Jordan is already a forceful,
rushing stream.

TRUST IN HIM

Trust in the Lord and do good;
live in the land and be safe.
Seek your happiness in the Lord,
and he will give you your heart's desire.

Give yourself to the Lord;
trust in him, and he will help you;
he will make your righteousness shine like the
noonday sun.
Be patient and wait for the Lord to act;
don't be worried about those who prosper or
those who succeed in their evil plans . . .

Those who trust in the Lord will possess the
land,
but the wicked will be driven out.

PSALM 37:3–7, 9

In the streets of the old city of Jerusalem.

LORD, I LOOK UP TO YOU

Lord, I look up to you,
up to heaven, where you rule.
As a servant depends on his master,
as a maid depends on her mistress,
so we will keep looking to you, O Lord our God,
until you have mercy on us.

Be merciful to us, Lord, be merciful;
we have been treated with so much contempt.
We have been mocked too long by the rich,
and scorned by proud oppressors.

PSALM 123

Keeping the sheep on the stony slopes of a hill in central
Turkey, near ancient Lystra.

HEAR MY CRY

From the depths of my despair I call to you,
Lord,
Hear my cry, O Lord;
listen to my call for help!
If you kept a record of our sins,
who could escape being condemned?
But you forgive us,
so that we should reverently obey you.

I wait eagerly for the Lord's help,
and in his word I trust.
I wait for the Lord
more eagerly than watchmen wait for the dawn—
than watchmen wait for the dawn.

Israel, trust in the Lord,
because his love is constant
and he is always willing to save.
He will save his people Israel
from all their sins.

PSALM 130

Light on the waters of one of the sources of the Jordan, at
Caesarea Philippi in northern Israel.

IN OLD AGE

Lord, I have come to you for protection;
never let me be defeated!
Because you are righteous, help me and
rescue me.
Listen to me and save me!
Be my secure shelter
and a strong fortress to protect me;
you are my refuge and defense.

My God, rescue me from wicked men,
from the power of cruel and evil men.
Sovereign Lord, I put my hope in you;
I have trusted in you since I was young.
I have relied on you all my life:
you have protected me since the day I was born.
I will always praise you.

PSALM 71:1–6

An old man watches the passersby at Tsefat, Israel.

GOD'S WORD

Your word, O Lord, will last forever;
it is eternal in heaven.
Your faithfulness endures through all the ages;
you have set the earth in place and it remains.
All things remain to this day because of your
command,
because they are all your servants.
If your law had not been the source of my joy,
I would have died from my sufferings.
I will never neglect your instructions,
because by them you have kept me alive.
I am yours—save me!
I have tried to obey your commands.
Wicked men are waiting to kill me,
but I will meditate on your laws.
I have learned that everything has limits;
but your commandment is perfect.

PSALM 119:89–96

Standing stone in the Negev desert.

AT PEACE

Lord, I have given up my pride,
and turned away from my arrogance.
I am not concerned with great matters
or with subjects too difficult for me.
Instead I am content and at peace.
As a child lies quietly in its mother's arms,
so my heart is quiet within me.
Israel, trust in the Lord
now and forever!

PSALM 131

Flocks graze peacefully as the sun sets over the hills of
Galilee.